EVERYTHING
MYTHOLOGY

NATIONAL
GEOGRAPHIC
KiDS

NATIONAL GEOGRAPHIC KiDS

EVERYTHING MYTHOLOGY

BY **BLAKE HOENA**

With National Geographic Explorer ADRIENNE MAYOR

Illustrated by GONZALO ORDOÑEZ and MARGARET SALTER

NATIONAL GEOGRAPHIC

WASHINGTON, D.C.

CONTENTS

Construction on the jungle temple complex of Angkor Wat in Cambodia began in 115 B.C., with temples dedicated to the Hindu god Vishnu. Over time, more than 100 temples were built with sculptures showing stories of Hindu and Buddhist religion and mythology.

In the mythology of the Algonquian people of North America, the Wendigo was a monster that could transform into a person. The Wendigo ate people and was never full.

INTRODUCTION

FROM THREE-HEADED
DOGS TO FIRE-BREATHING DRAGONS

and frost giants, myths are filled with incredible creatures. In these thrilling stories, there are also powerful gods such as Zeus, the Greek god of the sky, who cast lightning bolts down on people who angered him, and mighty heroes such as Heracles and Gilgamesh, who battled horrific beasts. Today, we think of myths as fantastic tales, but long ago, people believed they were more than simple stories. In the past, people from many cultures worshipped mythic gods. Some still do today. They tell the stories and celebrate the bold heroes who defied the gods and battled those horrible monsters. Today, myths are both a part of history and a part of living culture for many peoples throughout the world. So get ready to enter an amazing world where gods and terrifying monsters are real, and discover EVERYTHING about mythology.

EXPLORER'S CORNER

Hi! I'm Dr. Adrienne Mayor.

I research the meaning behind pre-scientific myths and oral stories, especially those about geology and other natural features. Known as geomyths, these stories are a kind of history of human curiosity. They show how ancient peoples, without science as we know it today, struggled to understand things. I like to study myths that provide insight into the natural artifacts from ancient cultures. I want to share with you how even long ago, people had a desire to understand the world around them.

The Greek Titan Prometheus was punished by the other gods for stealing fire and giving it to humans, allowing for human progress.

1
MYSTERY AND MAYHEM

WHAT IS A MYTH?

A STORY. THAT'S THE SIMPLE ANSWER. MYTHS ARE STORIES PEOPLE TELL EACH

other. But myths are more than just entertaining tales. Myths help people make sense of the world around them. In ancient times, people didn't have science like we have today to explain things. They didn't know what caused rain to fall from the sky or understand why the sun rose in the morning. The world was a mysterious place to them. Instead of science, people used myths to explain nature and how the world was created.

CREATION MYTHS

These myths explain how everything in the world came to be, from the sky and the Earth to all the living things. In creation myths, there is often a mother goddess or a creator god. They imagine a new world and use their powers to create it. In some Native American myths, the world started out as a place covered in water. The Great Spirit in the Iroquois creation myth sent down a woman to fill this world with people. There was no place for her to stand. So Beaver, one of the many animal spirits, suggested piling mud on Turtle's back to give her a place to live. The mud became an island. Turtle carried the island, Sky Woman, and her children on his back. Turtle Island became known as North America.

IT'S MYTHIC! GREEK AND ROMAN GODS PLACED HEROES IN THE SKY AS CONSTELLATIONS.

QUEST MYTHS

Everybody loves a hero who travels to faraway places and completes impossible tasks. Quest myths are hero myths. Heroes set out on quests to gain fame and riches, or to serve punishment from the gods. In European myths, Grendel, a hateful monster, terrorized Daneland. This beast slaughtered men simply because he was annoyed at the noise they made during the night. Beowulf, from the land of Geat, heard of Grendel's savagery. He traveled to Daneland and slayed the monster. In doing so, Beowulf earned fame and riches, and he eventually became the king of Geat.

NATURE MYTHS

Nature myths tell why things happen in nature, from the changing seasons to sunsets and stars. Nature myths also may tell why an animal possesses certain traits and abilities. In Greek and Roman myths, Arachne was a skilled weaver. Arachne even bragged that she was a better weaver than Athena, goddess of wisdom as well as weaving. Angered by Arachne's boastful words, Athena turned Arachne into a spider, but as a spider she kept her weaving skills. This myth explained to people why spiders weave their beautiful webs.

WHAT ISN'T A MYTH?

Many people think myths, legends, and folktales are the same thing. While they often overlap, myths attempt to explain the world, and the stories are often sacred. Legends are stories that claim to be true even though there is no proof. Folktales are beliefs and stories passed down from person to person.

SACRED SPACES

IN ANCIENT TIMES,
MYTHS AND RELIGION WERE OFTEN

one and the same. People worshipped the gods and spirits from mythology as if they truly existed and really controlled people's lives. In mythologies with many gods, each god had different powers. People prayed to the god or goddess who could help them. They also built temples to honor their gods or prayed at sacred spaces. Some of these places still exist. By learning about these places, we can understand how important mythic gods were to people's lives.

EXPLORER'S CORNER

In a way, temples were also museums. In them, people placed remarkable objects that they discovered or that seemed important to their gods. Some interesting things found in temples include bones of extinct mastodons that people thought were the remains of giants. They also include the ivory tusks of prehistoric mammoths believed to be from the Calydonian boar, which terrorized Greece. A large backbone found by the sea was exhibited as the remains of a great sea serpent.

CHOLULA PYRAMID

Quetzalcoatl, the feathered serpent god of Mesoamerican mythology, was a central god at Cholula, one of the largest pyramids in the world. Construction on this temple in southern Mexico began more than 2,000 years ago. In some Mesoamerican cultures, Quetzalcoatl was the god of light who taught people arts and crafts.

IT'S MYTHIC! ACCORDING TO A MYTH, THE GREEK GODS RULED FROM MOUNT OLYMPUS, THE HIGHEST PEAK IN GREECE.

SHIVA'S SHRINE

A shrine is a holy place where gods are worshipped. The town of Murudeshwara in south-west India is home to the second largest statue of the Hindu god Shiva, a main god who is sometimes called "the destroyer." The statue is part of an ancient shrine complex.

VALLEY OF THE KINGS

In eastern Egypt, along the western bank of the Nile, many pharoahs' tombs have been unearthed. Some are 3,500 years old. Ancient Egyptians viewed the pharaohs as gods and honored them by building tombs and pyramids. These structures weren't temples, but burial places that held a pharaoh's body and wealth so that he would have them in the afterlife.

ULURU

A natural sandstone formation in central Australia, Uluru (also called Ayers Rock) stands as tall as a skyscraper and is more than 5 miles (8 km) around. This massive rock is sacred to the Aboriginal people. They believe that by touching Uluru, they will receive blessings from their ancestral spirits.

BATTLES OF THE GODS

IN MOST MYTHOLOGIES,

THE GODS WERE ALWAYS RARING FOR A fight, whether it was to prove their might or defend their honor. Myths are filled with everything from godly squabbles to epic battles that pit the gods against each other. It was gods against monsters, or gods against people.

The strife between the gods was a reflection of life during ancient times. Wars and battles swept across the land, causing bloodshed and chaos. Empires rose and fell by the might of their armies. That's why gods of war were often one of the most powerful and feared gods in most mythologies. While people fought over land with swords and spears, the gods fought for control with supernatural powers that threatened to destroy the world.

HINDU GOD FAMILY FEUD

In Hindu mythology, the Deva gods were constantly at odds with their half brothers, the Asuras, and they fought 12 fierce battles.

OPPONENTS: Friendly Devas vs. demonic Asuras

WHY THEY FOUGHT: To decide whether good or evil would control the three worlds

BATTLE LOCATION: Earth, heaven, and the netherworld

TACTICS AND MANEUVERS: The gods fought on land and in cosmic oceans as serpents, dragons, and creatures that were half human and half lion.

LOSSES: Several avatars, gods, and relatives were killed before the Asuras were defeated in the 12th battle and became servants of the Devas.

TOOLS OF THE TRADE

While gods had unimaginable power, many had weapons or other items that served as their symbols of power.

SHIVA

(Hindu destroyer/transformer god) carried a trident, rode a bull, and wore serpents as decoration. This god practiced yoga, but was both a destroyer and a rebuilder.

THOR

(Norse god of thunder) wielded a magic war hammer, Mjölnir, that controlled lightning and always flew back to him after being thrown.

ZEUS

(Greek god of the sky) whose symbol was a thunderbolt, fought by throwing lightning bolts at his enemies or people who angered him.

OGUN

(African god of iron, knives, and war) wielded an iron machete.

The Norse, or Viking, god Odin fights the monstrous wolf Fenrir at the great Battle of Ragnarok.

FURY OF THE VIKING GODS

Ragnarok, the Day of Doom, was a devastating battle that destroyed the world. But have no fear, after this great world-ending brawl, everything was born again, fresh and new.

OPPONENTS: Gods against gods, gods against giants, and gods against monsters such as the wolf Fenrir

WHY THEY FOUGHT: Loki, the trickster god, killed Balder, the god of innocence and light.

BATTLE LOCATION: On the plain of Vigrid, in one of the nine worlds that Odin, the king of the gods, ruled over

TACTICS AND MANEUVERS: The gods fought a final pitched battle in which floods, darkness, fire, and earthquakes destroyed the world.

LOSSES: Norse gods were not immortal, and several died in battle, including Odin, Thor, Freyr, and Loki. But a few gods survived and lived on when the world was born again.

KU, THE HAWAIIAN WAR GOD, CAUSED LIGHT TO SHINE ON EARTH.

IT'S MYTHIC! THE GREEK WORD *MYTHOS* MEANS "STORY" OR "ANYTHING TOLD BY WORD OF MOUTH."

A WORLD OF MYTH

OFTEN, IT'S THE
ANCIENT GREEKS, ROMANS,
and Vikings we think about when it
comes to myths. After all, the planets
are all named after Roman gods.
Stories of Greek heroes Heracles and
Perseus, and Viking god Thor, who
slayed monsters, have been turned
into movies. Most cultures have their
own mythologies.

EXPLORER'S CORNER

Although mythologies from around the world
are unique in some ways, they also borrowed
from one another. We know of the griffin from
Greek myths, but this half-lion, half-eagle
creature was probably based on stories of a
magical beast told by the nomads of Central
Asia. *Protoceratops* fossils found in Mongolia
may be the origin of many griffin stories.
Protoceratops were dinosaurs that walked on
four legs and had sharp beaks. Their fossils
led people to imagine a creature that could
run on all fours yet had bird parts. Therefore
it could also fly, like the mythical griffin.

COYOTE

NORTH AMERICA

CANADA

UNITED STATES

MEXICO

GUATEMALA

CUBA

West Indies

BELIZE
HAITI
DOMINICAN
REPUBLIC
HONDURAS
EL SALVADOR

SURINAME

SOUTH AMERICA

NATIVE AMERICAN
Coyote is a trickster spirit
in many Native American
mythologies.

AZTEC CALENDAR

AZTEC
The Aztec may have used
calendars to divide time for
worshipping the gods.

MAYA
The Maya developed the first form
of writing in the Americas. Many
of their myths were recorded in a
book called *Popol Vuh,* including a
story about how the creator god,
Heart of Sky, made people from
maize, or corn.

MAYA GOD

MAP KEY

Highlighted areas on map
represent the historic boundaries
of where these cultures existed.

Note: Map shows present-day country
boundaries and names.

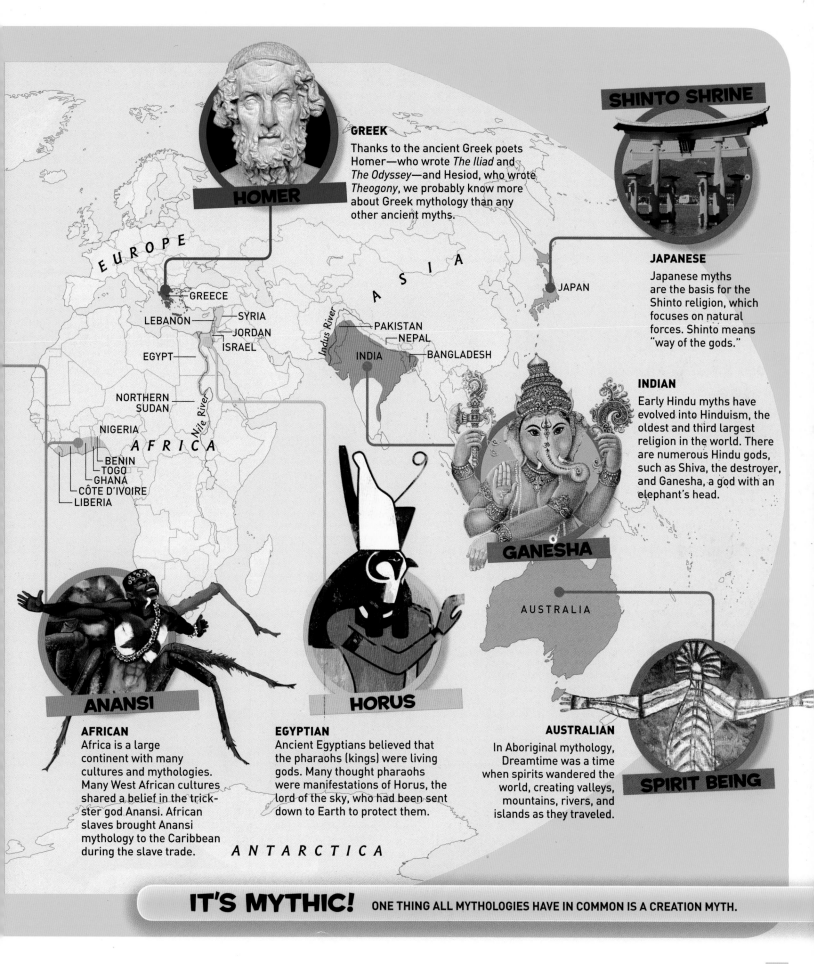

HOMER

GREEK
Thanks to the ancient Greek poets Homer—who wrote *The Iliad* and *The Odyssey*—and Hesiod, who wrote *Theogony*, we probably know more about Greek mythology than any other ancient myths.

SHINTO SHRINE

JAPANESE
Japanese myths are the basis for the Shinto religion, which focuses on natural forces. Shinto means "way of the gods."

INDIAN
Early Hindu myths have evolved into Hinduism, the oldest and third largest religion in the world. There are numerous Hindu gods, such as Shiva, the destroyer, and Ganesha, a god with an elephant's head.

GANESHA

ANANSI

AFRICAN
Africa is a large continent with many cultures and mythologies. Many West African cultures shared a belief in the trickster god Anansi. African slaves brought Anansi mythology to the Caribbean during the slave trade.

HORUS

EGYPTIAN
Ancient Egyptians believed that the pharaohs (kings) were living gods. Many thought pharaohs were manifestations of Horus, the lord of the sky, who had been sent down to Earth to protect them.

SPIRIT BEING

AUSTRALIAN
In Aboriginal mythology, Dreamtime was a time when spirits wandered the world, creating valleys, mountains, rivers, and islands as they traveled.

EUROPE
ASIA
AFRICA
ANTARCTICA

GREECE
LEBANON
SYRIA
JORDAN
ISRAEL
EGYPT
NORTHERN SUDAN
NIGERIA
BENIN
TOGO
GHANA
CÔTE D'IVOIRE
LIBERIA
Nile River
Indus River
PAKISTAN
NEPAL
INDIA
BANGLADESH
JAPAN
AUSTRALIA

IT'S MYTHIC! ONE THING ALL MYTHOLOGIES HAVE IN COMMON IS A CREATION MYTH.

AN ILLUSTRATED DIAGRAM

GODS OF OLYMPUS FAMILY TREE

IF YOU THINK SOME MODERN-DAY FAMILIES ARE confusing, with stepparents and half siblings, wait until you see the family tree of the gods of Olympus, home to the Greek gods. The family tree here includes some of the best known figures of Greek mythology, but the gods also had many children and grandchildren too numerous to mention here.

GAIA (GODDESS OF THE EARTH) + URANUS (GOD OF THE SKY)

THE TITANS

The Titans were the first powerful Greek gods. They were the children of Gaia and Uranus, and they ruled during a time called the Golden Age.

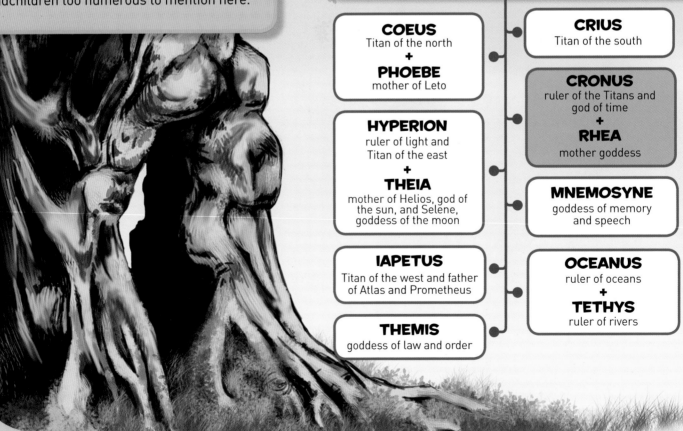

COEUS
Titan of the north
+
PHOEBE
mother of Leto

CRIUS
Titan of the south

HYPERION
ruler of light and
Titan of the east
+
THEIA
mother of Helios, god of
the sun, and Selene,
goddess of the moon

CRONUS
ruler of the Titans and
god of time
+
RHEA
mother goddess

MNEMOSYNE
goddess of memory
and speech

IAPETUS
Titan of the west and father
of Atlas and Prometheus

OCEANUS
ruler of oceans
+
TETHYS
ruler of rivers

THEMIS
goddess of law and order

CRONUS + RHEA

THE OLYMPIANS

Titans Cronus and Rhea had six children, who became the gods and goddesses of Olympus.

ZEUS
god of the sky

HERA
goddess of marriage and childbirth

POSEIDON
god of the sea

HADES
ruler of the underworld

HESTIA
goddess of the home and family

DEMETER
goddess of the harvest

POSEIDON

HERA

CHILDREN OF ZEUS

Zeus fathered so many gods, goddesses, demigods (half god, half human), and heroes that it is hard to keep them straight. Here are just some of his best known children.

PERSEUS
a hero

HERACLES
(HERCULES)
the strongest of all mortals

APOLLO
an olympian and god of the arts and the sun

HELEN OF TROY
the most beautiful woman in the world

HERMES
(MERCURY)
an olympian and messenger of the gods

APHRODITE
(VENUS)
an olympian and goddess of love

ARTEMIS
Apollo's Twin, goddess of the hunt, and Healer god

ZEUS AND **HERA** WERE MARRIED.

The hero Theseus was a half-god who slayed the Minotaur, a half-man, half-bull monster. The Minotaur lived in a mazelike home called the labyrinth.

2

GODS AND HEROES

A GOD'S LIFE

YOU MIGHT THINK
POSSESSING THE POWER OF THE GODS

would be really cool. But with great power came great responsibility. Not all gods were up to the work. Despite their supernatural abilities, gods had character flaws and problems. Some were jealous. Many were spoiled, demanding sacrifices and worship. When they didn't get what they wanted, they became nasty and had tantrums.

A PANTHEON IS A GROUP OF THE GODS FROM ONE CULTURE.

MMM, TASTY CHILDREN

Cronus, the ruler of the Titans in Greek mythology, was so nasty that he ate his own children, not because they were tasty, but because he was afraid they would overthrow him and take his throne. Cronus swallowed each of his children right after they were born. Rhea, mother of the children, wasn't happy about Cronus eating her babies, so she played a trick on him. When Zeus was born, she gave Cronus a rock covered in blankets to eat instead of her son. The trick worked, and Zeus escaped death. Later, Zeus slipped poison into Cronus's food, causing him to vomit the rest of his kids. Zeus then escaped with his brothers and sisters, freed the Cyclopes and some giants, and together they overthrew Cronus and the Titans.

Cronus ate his children. As immortals, they did not die and were just trapped in his belly.

IT'S MYTHIC! IN MANY MYTHOLOGIES, GODS APPEARED AS PEOPLE OR ANIMALS.

> Cemeteries and graveyards are for mortals. Gods live forever.

MYTHIC PETS

Like us, the gods had their pets. They may not have had a ball-chasing boxer or tweeting parakeets, but they had pets—loving, obedient, pet-at-your-own-risk sort of pets.

CERBERUS

Here Doggy Doggy . . . Cerberus guarded the gates of Hades, and no mortal could sneak by this vicious dog because it had three heads.

AQUILA

Ouch, My Liver! As god of the sky, Zeus had a pet eagle, Aquila. It often exacted Zeus's punishment, such as ripping out the god Prometheus's liver on a daily basis.

SLEIPNIR

The Fastest Ride in Town! The Norse god Odin couldn't ride just any old nag. His horse, Sleipnir, had eight legs!

A MERE MORTAL

Most gods can live forever. Some gods die but are later reborn. But mortals have a time limit. Mortals are humans, and all humans die at some point. In Greek and Roman mythology, a demigod is the child of a god and a human. Their god half makes demigods stronger and braver than full mortals, but like mortals, they can die. Demigods are also more kindhearted and loyal than gods. In Hindu mythology, demigods are humans who became gods.

WHEN HORSES FLY

What do you get when you combine a god of the sea with a snake-headed monster? A flying horse! Pegasus, the horse with wings, is the foal of Medusa and sea god Poseidon. The winged white stallion was also the trusty steed of Greek hero Bellerophon. A slayer of monsters, Bellerophon killed three-headed, fire-breathing Chimera.

NOBLE BIRD-LION

Half bird, half lion, the griffin of European mythology was a powerful and noble creature. A true king of beasts, the griffin had a head and front of an eagle, and the back legs and tail of a lion. It guarded treasure and mated for life.

FLUTE-PLAYING GOATS

Satyrs had goatlike legs and feet, and the upper bodies of men. They were the companions of the Greek god of the grape harvest, Dionysus, as they were musically inclined and loved wine. They are often pictured playing flutes.

MAGICAL CREATURES

MYTHOLOGIES ARE JAM-PACKED
WITH WEIRD, WACKY, AND MYSTERIOUS MAGICAL

creatures. Where did the ideas for some magical creatures in myths come from? That is often a mystery, as many of these creatures seem to be just a jumble of animal parts. Unlike monsters, magical creatures helped the gods and people (or at least they didn't try to eat them).

BURP! EXCUSE THE RAINBOW

In African myths, Bunzi was a cosmic snake that brought forth rain, and in some stories, a python was said to belch out the rainbows after a storm. Snakes were also symbols of rebirth, because they shed their skins and were thought to live forever.

PART BIRD, PART GOD

Garuda is the birdlike Hindu god that the god Vishnu rode. As if gods riding other gods isn't confusing enough, Garuda also has at least 12 other names and often wears serpents on his wrists and as a belt. He represents the sun and fire.

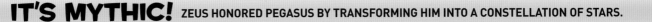

IT'S MYTHIC! ZEUS HONORED PEGASUS BY TRANSFORMING HIM INTO A CONSTELLATION OF STARS.

AN ARROW TO THE HEART

WHERE WOULD THE GODS AND HEROES BE

WITHOUT LOVE? PROBABLY IN A LOT LESS TROUBLE! LOVE AND PASSION drove gods wild and led to some interesting mythical adventures. Strong emotions, such as love, hate, anger, and jealousy, are hard to control. Stories of the gods of love and war show how disastrous these emotions can be if unchecked.

Love By the Numbers

3 Erotes, or lesser gods of love, help and advise the goddess Aphrodite.

4 known temples are dedicated to Hathor, the Egyptian goddess of love and motherhood.

8 Aztec gods and goddesses are dedicated to love and passion.

10 major and minor Greek goddesses and gods are dedicated to love.

13 names are known for Kamadeva, the Hindu god of love.

LOVE WAGES WAR

One of the greatest mythical love stories is that of Helen of Troy, the most beautiful woman in the world. She was married to the Greek king Menelaus. Aphrodite, the Greek goddess of love, promised her to Paris, a prince of Troy, if Paris would only say that Aphrodite was more beautiful than Hera and Athena. Paris whisked Helen away (above). Menelaus gathered a Greek army to get her back. The Greeks won after they hid themselves in a large wooden horse. The Trojans brought the horse into the city. The Greek soldiers snuck out of the horse, opened the gates to the city, and then defeated Troy.

IT'S MYTHIC! ANYONE STRUCK BY CUPID'S ARROWS FELL IN LOVE WITH THE NEXT PERSON (OR BEAST) THEY SAW.

VENUS: ROMAN GODDESS OF LOVE

Her name alone conjures images of beauty, and there's even a planet named after her! A favorite of artists, the Roman goddess of love, Venus, is the mother of Cupid (painting "The Birth of Venus" by Sandro Botticelli, above). Many have vied for her affections, including the cranky god of fire, Vulcan. Their marriage was considered a war of love and fire. Venus was said to be born of a clam shell.

LOVE AND CATS?

Freya, the Norse, or Viking goddess of love and beauty, is also the goddess of war and death. When traveling, Freya rides a chariot pulled by two cats (above)! She wears a cloak of falcon feathers and has a magical necklace. Freya helps those in love and also brings half of those who die in battle to the afterlife.

CUPID'S ARROW

The Roman god Cupid is often depicted as a winged cherub or young boy with a bow and arrow (right). When hit by Cupid's arrow, people are filled with love for another person. He also carries a torch, which represents how love wounds and inflames the heart.

EXPLORER'S CORNER

In myths, the Amazons were a race of warrior women, both beautiful and dangerous—they were actually inspired by real Scythian (western Asian) nomadic women who were expert archers. Heroes from Heracles to Theseus and Achilles fell in love and fought with Amazon queens. And myths of these brave, independent, and lovely warriors raised questions about whether women could be the equals of men.

GREEN GOD OF LOVE

Kamadeva, the Hindu god of love and desire (above), is young, handsome, and green-skinned. He carries a sugarcane bow, and his arrows are fragrant flowers. He is considered a warrior of love and rides a bird.

HEROES TO THE RESCUE

SOME OF THE MOST EXCITING
MYTHS INVOLVE HEROES BATTLING MONSTERS

during daring and dangerous adventures or quests. These stories served a purpose in ancient myth: They taught people about bravery and discovery. Quest myths also were a way of showing people that they could take control of their lives. If heroes could be brave facing impossible tasks and mighty gods, then ordinary people didn't need to be so afraid of a little thunder.

TOKOYO SAVES THE DAY!

In Japanese myths Yofune-nushi was a fiery-eyed sea serpent with glowing scales. It ruled the waters near the Oki Islands. Every year it demanded the sacrifice of a young woman. If Yofune-nushi didn't receive its meal, the serpent would raise storms and destroy fishing boats. One year, the heroine Tokoyo volunteered to be the sacrifice. She waited for Yofune-nushi near the monster's lair, and when the unsuspecting serpent appeared, she stabbed it in the eye with a dagger. Yofune-nushi tried to escape, but Tokoyo kept up her attack and killed the beast.

EVEN HEROES NEED HELP

While some heroes were children of the gods and gifted with special abilities, often they still needed a little help on their quest, and most mythologies had a god who fought to protect people. In Greek mythology, that goddess was Athena. People know her as the goddess of wisdom and war, but her most important role was as the protector of heroes.

THE LABORS OF HERACLES

Heracles was the favorite son of Zeus, which angered Hera, because he was Zeus's son with a mortal woman. At one point, Hera caused Heracles to go mad, and he accidently killed his family. In order to gain forgiveness from the gods for this horrific deed, he was assigned 12 nearly impossible tasks.

TO DO LIST

- ☑ Slay the Nemean lion, whose skin could not be pierced by arrows. After slaying the lion with his bare hands, Heracles used its hide as a protective cloak.
- ☑ Kill the nine-headed Hydra (below), a serpent-like water creature.
- ☑ Catch the Ceryneian hind, an incredibly swift deer.
- ☑ Kill the Erymanthian boar, a giant boar.
- ☑ Clean out the Augean stables, which were filled with 30 years' worth of horse manure.
- ☑ Drive away the flock of deadly Stymphalian birds.
- ☑ Defeat the Cretan bull, father of the Minotaur.
- ☑ Round up the mares of Diomedes, who were man-eating horses.
- ☑ Steal the belt from Hippolyta, the queen of the mighty Amazons, a tribe of female warriors.
- ☑ Take the cattle from Geryon, a giant with three bodies, three heads, and six hands and feet.
- ☑ Find the secret garden where the apples of the Hesperides grow.
- ☑ Defeat Cerberus, the three-headed dog that guarded the underworld's gate.

THESEUS SLAYS THE BULL—WITH HELP

Heroes may have had all the brawn, but often they would have been lost without a heroine's smarts. Every nine years, the city of Athens sent 14 tributes to Crete, where King Minos had them thrown into the Minotaur's Labyrinth. This half-man, half-bull monster feasted on the people who wandered around lost in its endless maze. One year, Theseus volunteered to be one of the tributes. Even though he was the son of a god, he never would have survived if it wasn't for Ariadne, King Minos's daughter. She felt sorry for Theseus, and before he entered the Labyrinth, she gave him a spool of thread to mark his way through the maze. Once Theseus defeated the Minotaur, Ariadne was there to unlock the door to the Labyrinth so he could escape back home.

The Hydra could regrow its heads and had poisonous blood!

IT'S MYTHIC! MANY HEROES WERE HALF GOD AND HALF MORTAL.

A PHOTO GALLERY

MYTHOLOGY IN ART

MYTHICAL GODS
AND MONSTERS MAKE

excellent subjects for art and architecture. Even today, these symbols of our past are seen in public statues and sculptures, in art museums, and on the street on T-shirts and tattoos.

Hades, god of the Greek underworld, is often depicted with Cerberus, the three-headed guard dog.

The Pallas Athena fountain in Vienna, Austria, honors the Greek goddess of wisdom, law, and justice.

A gilded statue of Prometheus at New York City's Rockefeller Center in the United States

The Dragon Bridge is in Ljubljana, capital city of Slovenia. Legend has it that the city was founded by the ancient Greek hero Jason, who killed dragons on a quest.

Atlas was an early Greek god who was sentenced by Zeus to forever hold the heavens upon his shoulders.

In the mythology of the Maori, the native people of New Zealand, a god stick could be stuck in the ground and used as a temporary shrine for a god.

The one-eyed Cyclops Polyphemus was a giant who liked to eat men. He was tricked by the hero Odysseus, who blinded him to escape certain death.

3
THE DARK SIDE

TRICKSTERS

EVERYONE KNOWS A
TRICKSTER—THAT GUY OR GIRL
who can't follow the rules and loves to play jokes. In most mythologies, a trickster is a god, goddess, or spirit who enjoys playing tricks on gods and mortals alike. Sometimes, tricksters like to spite the other gods in order to help people. The trickster is often punished by the other gods.

LIGHT MY FIRE

In myths, the first people made by the creator god are often innocent and ignorant. They are happy to exist and worship the gods. Then some trickster god comes along and teaches people a thing or two that ruins the bliss. In Greek myths, that god was Prometheus, the Titan of culture and intelligence. He looked down from the heavens and saw humans struggling to survive. So he stole fire from the Olympians and offered it to people. With fire, people were less reliant on the gods, a fact that angered Zeus. Prometheus was chained to a mountain, and every day a bird tore out his liver. The liver grew back each night, meaning the torture was endless.

IT'S MYTHIC! IN MANY NATIVE AMERICAN MYTHS, CROW IS THE TRICKSTER WHO GIVES PEOPLE FIRE.

THANKS FOR THE SHOWER!

In western Africa, Anansi, the god of knowledge and stories, is a popular trickster god. In one myth, Nyame, the sky god, creates the hot sun. Anansi tricks Nyame into sending rain down to Earth to cool people off.

DEVIOUS LOKI

The Norse trickster god was Loki. And while Prometheus and Coyote helped people, Loki was a bit more devious. He could change shapes, even looking like other gods or changing gender to confuse people. In one myth, Loki helps steal the apples of Idun, the goddess of eternal youth. Without her apples, the gods would grow old and die.

WILY COYOTE

Coyote is a trickster god found in many Native American myths. He is also said to have given humans the gift of fire. In many mythologies, the trickster god has a close relationship with the Creator god. So when the Creator decided to flood the world and rid it of the first people, Coyote went against the Creator and decided to help the people. He told them to build a big canoe to prepare for the flood.

MONSTERS OF MYTH

POISONOUS BREATH?
BLOOD THAT BURNS? A FACE THAT
could kill you just by looking at it? The monsters of myth are the stuff of nightmares. What would a hero do if there weren't horrifying monsters and deadly creatures to battle? Some mythical monsters were the children of gods. Greek creator gods Gaia and Uranus not only birthed the Titans, but also many other creatures, one more monstrous than the next. Other monsters were created by vengeful gods to harm mortals.

TYPHON

Lair: A cave in ancient Greece

Parents: Gaia and Tartarus

Enemies: Zeus and all the gods

Probably the deadliest and most dangerous monster in Greek mythology, Typhon is sometimes called the father of monsters. He and his wife Echidna birthed many of the horrific creatures that heroes had to slay, including Chimera, Cerberus, the Nemean lion, and the Sphinx. Typhon's eyes flashed fire and his hands and lower body were a mass of hissing snakes.

THE **NOBUSUMA** IS A **FLYING SQUIRREL MONSTER** IN **JAPANESE MYTHOLOGY.**

IT'S MYTHIC! MEDUSA WAS SO HORRIBLE TO LOOK UPON THAT PEOPLE WERE PETRIFIED BY FEAR.

CHIMERA

Lair: Ancient Turkey

Parents: Echidna and Typhon, two monstrous children of Gaia and Uranus

Foe: Greek hero Bellerophon

Power: Fiery breath and a vicious bite

Probably one of the oddest-looking monsters in myth, Chimera had the head of a lion in front, from which it breathed fire, the head of a goat sprouting from its middle, and the head of a dragon or snake at the tip of its tail.

MINOTAUR

Lair: Labyrinth of Crete, a Greek island

Parents: Cretan bull and Pasiphae, Queen of Crete

Foe: Theseus, son of god Poseidon and the first prince of Athens

Power: Brute strength

This half-man, half-bull monster roams the Labyrinth of Crete. Should you wander into his lair, you will be lost forever. That is, until the Minotaur finds you and makes a meal of you.

QILIN

Lair: A garden

Parents: Unknown

Foe: Those who do wicked things

Power: Fiery breath

Qilin killed people who were mean to good people. If you threatened a saintly person, this dragon-headed horse would fry you to a crisp.

POLYPHEMUS, A CYCLOPS

Lair: Cave on the island of Sicily

Parents: Greek god Poseidon and Thoosa, a sea nymph

Foe: Greek hero Odysseus

Power: Good aim with a rock

For fun, one-eyed Polyphemus likes to chuck rocks at passing ships, and then munch on the shipwrecked sailors as they swim to shore.

Monsters By the Numbers

1 eye grew in the forehead of a Cyclops.

8 legged horse Sleipnir was the trusty steed companion of Norse god Odin.

9 hideous heads on the serpent sea creature Hydra grew back each time they were cut off.

12 heads on the sea monster Scylla were divided evenly between dog heads and monster heads.

50 feet (15 m) in length is the size of a giant squid—the real-life equivalent of the sea monster the Kraken.

DREADFUL DISASTERS

VOLCANOES, FLOODS, AND

EARTHQUAKES ARE JUST A FEW OF THE
natural disasters that ancient peoples chalked up to the anger
of the gods. Can you blame them? There weren't any meteorolo-
gists or weather forecasters at the time. Disasters, whether
natural or human-made, were a mystery. People didn't know
why they occurred, and they often blamed a vengeful god, such
as Poseidon, who could create earthquakes with his trident.

GREAT BALLS OF FIRE

Vulcan was the Roman god of fire, volcanoes, blacksmiths, cooks, and
bakers. Romans celebrated him every August 23 with the festival of
Vulcanalia. If there was an ancient tourist brochure for Vulcanalia, it
might have promoted the sacrifice of small animals and possibly a big
red bull in bonfires throughout Rome. Everybody would be there, since
Vulcanalia was *the* event of the late summer in ancient Rome.

EXPLORER'S CORNER

Geomythology, an emerging discipline of study, investigates early
myths that show a genuine knowledge and understanding about
natural phenomena, such as earthquakes, floods, tsunamis, and
volcanoes—the very things behind many mythic disasters. Geomyths
are not truly scientific. They tell of natural events in mythical terms,
with gods and monsters as their cause. Amazingly, they often provide
accurate details of natural catastrophes such as volcanoes, earthquakes, floods, explosions of gases, and tsunamis that happened
thousands of years ago.

AND THEN THE EARTH SHOOK

Japan has a lot of earthquakes. In Japanese mythology, Kashima-no-kami (right) is the god of thunder and swords. He is also reputed to be the cause of earthquakes. Or rather, his giant catfish, Namazu, causes them. Namazu lives in the mud under Japan, and Kashima restrains him with a stone. Every once in a while, Kashima gets distracted, and Namazu thrashes to free himself, causing earthquakes.

NEREIDS WERE **SEA NYMPHS** WHO **HELPED SAILORS** LOST IN **SEA STORMS.**

DON'T OPEN THAT BOX!

The myth of Pandora explains all the evil that is in the world. Angry at people for taking Prometheus's gift of fire, Zeus gave Pandora, the first human created by gods, a box filled with many things, such as all the evils in the world. He told Pandora never to open the box. But with the gift of fire came knowledge and curiosity, and eventually Pandora couldn't resist. She lifted the box's lid and out escaped disease, conflict, work, and other troubles that would plague people.

IT'S MYTHIC! THE HAWAIIAN FIRE GODDESS PELE LIVES IN THE KILAUEA VOLCANO.

THE UNDERWORLD

NOBODY ESCAPES

DEATH—IT'S PRETTY MUCH A guarantee. But in mythology, the dead have a place to go and a god or a caretaker to look after them. Most mythologies had an afterlife, or a place where the dead lived on in some form. The afterlife was often a place of judgment, where the ruler of the underworld determined what would happen to a person's soul.

LET ME IN!

Not only was Hades the name of the ruler of the Greek underworld, but it was also the name of the land of the dead. Not everyone who died got into Hades. A coin had to be placed into a dead person's mouth. This coin paid the toll for the ferryman Charon. The River Styx separated Earth from the underworld, and Charon ferried souls across the river, but only if they paid his toll. The Greek underworld was made up of several places. Some were for punishment, such as the River Acheron, which was the river of pain. Other places, the Elysian Fields, rewarded brave heroes. The worst place to be in the underworld was the deep dark dungeon Tartarus, where monsters and creatures were locked away by the Titans.

A view of Hades, the Greek underworld, where its ruler and three-headed guard dog await the ferryman bringing souls across the River Styx

IT'S MYTHIC! THE GREEK UNDERWORLD WAS A DARK AND MURKY PLACE.

Valkyries are women on winged horses who bring brave men who die in battle to the Viking hall of Valhalla.

HALL OF THE SLAIN

In Norse mythology, the myths of the Vikings, Valhalla is a great hall in the world of Asgard where brave warriors go when they die. Odin, the king of the gods, rules over Valhalla. Mortals and gods are led to Valhalla by Valkyries, women on winged horses. Half of those who die are chosen by the Valkyries. The rest go to Folkvangre with the goddess Freya.

But that's only the beginning of the end, and Valhalla and Folkvangre are just two of many underworlds. The dead warriors in Valhalla and Folkvangre drink honey wine and wait to fight in the great battle called Ragnarok, where the old world is destroyed and a new world emerges.

WEIGHING SOUL

In ancient Egyptian mythology, the afterlife ... would go with all their earthly possessions. But first, the de... ...urvive in the underworld among demons and jackal-headed ... the afterlife (second from left). Anubis helped weigh the truth in people's ... ...ned their fates. Good people had light hearts and a happy afterlife. ... ...rts heavy from their bad deeds. Their souls were eaten by Ammit, a mons... ...odile face.

MYTH-TAKEN IDENTITY

MYTH VS. REAL LIFE

EVER LOOK AT THE SKY AND SEE ANIMAL shapes in the clouds? Or a person's face in a knot of wood? Or something scary in a shadow? Experts believe many of the monsters and creatures in myth were based on real things people witnessed in nature. Some creatures from ancient myths weren't the beasts people thought they were. Rather, a fear of the unknown probably led to their mistaken identity.

DRAGON OR DINOSAUR?

Asia has a wealth of fossil deposits. When ancient people stumbled on the remains of dinosaurs, they were probably amazed by the size of the bones. But they didn't know what dinosaurs were, so the bones were most likely the source of dragons in myths.

HORSING AROUND

If you had never seen a person on a horse before, you might think a horseback rider was actually a half-horse, half-man creature. That is a likely source for Centaurs. Just look at the shadow of a person riding a horse. Does it look like one creature or two?

MY, WHAT LONG TENTACLES YOU HAVE

Krakens were large sea monsters with many tentacles. In myths, they attacked and sank ships. But in reality, people may have seen giant squids or large octopuses and believed them to be monsters.

A REAL BEAUTY

Manatees are slow-moving, graceful swimmers with humanlike eyes. They are one likely source for the belief in mermaids, or women with fishtails.

DON'T POKE ME

Narwhals are whales with a single horn (actually a tusk, or tooth) sticking out from their heads. Perhaps narwhals inspired the belief in unicorns. Myths say that Poseidon, Greek god of the sea, created horses.

The Hindu god Ganesha has the head of an elephant and four arms. He is known as a remover of obstacles and a lover of the arts.

4
FUN WITH
MYTHS

NEVER ENDING STORIES

EVEN THOUGH MYTHS ARE STORIES
FROM MANY YEARS AGO, THEY CONTINUE TO ENTERTAIN US

today. It's not just the original tales of heroes like Heracles and Gilgamesh that fascinate us. The myths from ancient times have been retold by modern-day writers in their own exciting ways. Don't believe it? Take a look at some popular books and movies.

MODERN STORY: THE HUNGER GAMES

In *The Hunger Games,* a top-selling book and movie series, 12 districts were defeated by the powerful central government. Every year 24 children, one boy and one girl from each district, are chosen as tributes to battle in the "games" in order to appease the central government. Katniss, the story's heroine, volunteers to be one of the tributes.

ANCIENT MYTH: THESEUS

Athens was defeated by Crete, and to appease the king of Crete, every nine years, seven boys and seven girls from Athens are chosen as tributes to enter the Labyrinth and become Minotaur meals. Theseus, the story's hero, volunteers to be one of the tributes (and with help, he kills the Minotaur).

MODERN STORY: SUPERHERO THOR

The Norse god of thunder and the protector of mankind made his first comic book appearance in 1962. He has since joined the Avengers, a team of superheroes who protect Earth from evil villains and powerful aliens, and starred in several hit movies.

ANCIENT MYTH: GOD OF THUNDER

In Norse mythology, Thor is the handsome red-haired god of thunder, lightning, storms, and strength. He wields a hammer, wears a magic belt and iron gloves, and with the help of his fellow gods, protects humankind from monstrous serpents.

IT'S MYTHIC! GREEK MYTHS WERE WRITTEN AS LONG POEMS.

MODERN STORY: PERCY JACKSON

In the top-selling book and movie series *Percy Jackson and the Olympians: The Lightning Thief*, Percy is the son of a god, Poseidon, and has several run-ins with the Titan Atlas, who is the commander of Cronus's army.

ANCIENT MYTH: PERSEUS

Perseus is the son of a god, Zeus, and during his quest to slay Medusa, he also has a run-in with Atlas, who once commanded Cronus's army.

MODERN STORY: THREE-HEADED HOUND

In the first book and movie of the Harry Potter series, *Harry Potter and the Sorcerer's Stone*, Hagrid gets a three-headed dog from a Greek man and names it Fluffy. Fluffy guards a chamber where the Sorcerer's Stone is kept. To get past Fluffy, Harry Potter lulls the beast to sleep by playing a flute.

ANCIENT MYTH: THREE-HEADED HOUND

In Greek mythology, the three-headed dog Cerberus guarded the entrance to the underworld. The musician Orpheus traveled to the underworld to see his dead wife. He lulled Cerberus to sleep by playing the harp.

SUPERHEROES

Most modern-day superheroes are based on mythic figures. Who might these heroes be today?

 HERACLES—the strongest man in myths.

 ACHILLES—his skin can't be pierced by weapons, but he has one weak spot: his ankle.

 ATLANTA—the fastest person alive in myths, she could outrun anyone.

A

IRON MAN
Tougher than bullets

B

THE FLASH
Fast as lightning

C

SUPERMAN
Strong as steel

CREATE A CREATURE

THREE HEADS ARE

BETTER THAN ONE, RIGHT? THE STORIES of mythology have all sorts of fantastic creatures with three heads and multiple arms. Often these beings appear to be a strange mix of different animals, such as the Sphinx, which had the body of a lion, the wings of a bird, and the face of a woman.

Bust out your colored pencils and notepad to create your own mythic creature. Answer these questions first and then let the drawing begin.

BODY BUILDING

HOOVES OR CLAWS?

What type of body does your creature have? Is it a human, fish, horse, cat, dog, rabbit, cow, elephant, spider, snake, or another favorite animal?

WINGS OR TAILS?

How does your creature get around? Does it have wings to fly? Does it swim with a fishtail or slither across the ground like a snake? Does it burrow under the ground with shovel-like hands for digging? Or is there another way it can get around?

WEAPON?

How does your creature get into battle mode? Does it carry a sword or a club in its hands? Does it breathe fire with a dragon's head? Does it bite with sharp teeth like a lion's or have a venomous bite like a snake's?

TISK TUSK

In ancient Hindu mythology, Airavata is a white elephant with seven trunks and four tusks. The god Indra rode Airavata into battle.

A CENTAUR IS HALF MAN AND HALF HORSE.

IT'S MYTHIC! GAIA WAS A MOTHER GODDESS. HER NAME MEANS "EARTH" IN THE GREEK LANGUAGE.

NAME YOUR BEAST!

Start with your first name. Then, along with your name, list on one line all the animal parts you used to make up your creature. Keep the first and last letters, but knock out some of the letters in the middle of the list to shorten your creature's name.

For example, the author of this book created a creature with three heads—one wolf, one shark, and one hawk head; a human body; and the tail of a snake for slithering around.

So that equals—Blakewolfsharkhawkpersonsnake.

Or for short, it's a Blawoshawkhunake.

Lastly, have fun drawing (just don't draw in this book)!

ARE YOU A GODDESS, GOD, OR HERO?

As far as jobs go, all are fantastic. Use this handy list of questions to determine which one you might want to have, and then tally your score.

1 **Are you drawn to adventure or excitement?**
If you answered yes, give yourself 3 points.

2 **Do you like your friends to follow you and do what you tell them to do?**
If you answered yes, give yourself 1 point.

3 **Do you feel you have to prove yourself to others?**
If you answered yes, give yourself 2 points.

4 **Are you easily bored?**
If you answered yes, give yourself 2 points.

5 **When you travel, you like to:**
A. Travel in style, stay at the best hotels, and eat well. If you answered yes, give yourself 2 points.
B. Go the budget route, sleep on a rock, and go fishing for food. If you answered yes, give yourself 4 points.

6 **When your friend asks for help, you:**
A. Say "Sorry bud, no can do. I've got important business to attend to!" If you answered yes, give yourself 1 point.
B. Say "I'll be right there." If you answered yes, give yourself 3 points.

7 **You prefer to wear:**
A. Torn sweatpants, sneakers, and a football jersey. If you answered yes, give yourself 2 points.
B. The latest cool fashions. If you answered yes, give yourself 1 point.

8 **Your neighbor's dog has run away and you:**
A. Ignore it. It's not your problem. Give yourself 1 point.
B. Organize a search party to find him and bring him back. If you answered yes, give yourself 3 points.
C. Wait until your neighbor asks for help and then offer help, but only if your neighbor makes you a sandwich first. If you answered yes, give yourself 2 points.

SCORING:

Fewer than 13 points—Congratulations, you are simply divine! Gods don't travel cheap, suffer for a cause, or help a worshipper unless they feel like it.

More than 13 points—Oh my hero, you have proven yourself uncomplaining, hardworking, and someone who can be counted on.

EAT LIKE A GOD

THE GODS WERE A

BUSY GROUP. WHEN NOT FIGHTING and meddling in the lives of mortals, they sat around at fancy banquets. You would think they would be feasting on all sorts of scrumptious food, but the gods of Olympus ate and drank only two things: ambrosia and nectar, a sweet drink made from honey.

FOOD OF THE GODS

The Greek gods did not eat mortal food because mortal food rots and dies. Ambrosia was said to be nine times sweeter than honey. It also smelled divine and could be eaten or drunk, while nectar was drunk. Ambrosia and nectar were brought to the gods by a nymph, and only gods could consume it. Mortals and demigods were not allowed to eat ambrosia, possibly because of its magical quality of giving the gods great strength.

THE GOD OF MAIZE (CORN), CENTEOTL, WAS VERY IMPORTANT TO THE AZTEC.

Images of gods of the Hindu pantheon adorn a temple. Temples often have offerings. Food offered to the Hindu gods is called *prasada*.

IT'S MYTHIC! DIONYSUS IS THE GREEK GOD OF WINE. THE ROMANS RENAMED HIM BACCHUS.

LETTUCE DRINK MILK!

Gods from many cultures ate and loved mortal food, and many gods were worshipped for their help in growing and making food. The Egyptian god Set had a love for lettuce, while Hindu god Dharmathakur ate only white foods such as rice, milk, and chicken. Most cultures had gods of food, feasting, the harvest, and wine. The Maya god Ixcacao was the goddess of cacao, or chocolate, and the Maya honored her with an offering of chocolate. The Japanese rice god, Inari, had a day devoted to his worship when rice transplanting festivals were held. Bacchus, the Roman god of wine, was also the god of good cheer and humor. Each March, Romans held a two-day festival in his honor, called the Bacchanalia.

Bacchus was also the Roman god of madness.

MAKE YOUR OWN AMBROSIA

Ambrosia is the name of a delectable fruit salad made with pineapple and mandarin oranges. You can make your own ambrosia using the fruits favored by ancient gods. Dates, figs, pomegranates, and honey were eaten by or offered to the gods of ancient Rome, Greece, and Egypt. They were all said to have magical properties. Ask an adult for permission and to help you use a knife for chopping.

YOU'LL NEED:

A large bowl, a measuring cup, spoons to measure and mix
1 cup fresh or canned pineapple chunks
1 cup mandarin orange slices
2 fresh dates, cut into bite-size chunks
3 dried figs, cut into bite-size chunks
½ cup pomegranate seeds
2 cups plain, unsweetened Greek yogurt
2 tablespoons honey
2 tablespoons unsweetened coconut flakes

DIRECTIONS: Mix the fruits in a bowl with the yogurt and honey. Add the coconut flakes. Stir and serve.

POMEGRANATES

HONEY

DATES

FIGS

LOOK TO THE HEAVENS

YOU ONLY HAVE TO LOOK TO

THE NIGHT SKY TO SEE THAT MYTHS HAVE FOREVER influenced our lives. Not only are the planets named after gods, along with other celestial bodies, but many of the constellations are based on figures from myth. Step outside on a clear night, and the following constellations should be easy to spot year-round.

URSA MAJOR (BIG BEAR) & URSA MINOR (LITTLE BEAR)

Sometimes called the Big Dipper and the Little Dipper, these constellations can be seen circling the northern part of the sky. Zeus put them up in the heavens to protect them from hunters. The bears have extremely long tails because he threw them into the heavens by their tails.

IT'S MYTHIC! AGRICULTURE GODS WERE IMPORTANT TO MANY CULTURES.

CASSIOPEIA

This queen insulted Poseidon's sea nymphs, so as her ultimate punishment, the god of the sea placed her upside down in the heavens where she sits tied to a chair. Her constellation looks like a large *w*.

NAME THAT PLANET

Many planets are named for Roman or Greek gods, goddesses, and mythic beings:

MERCURY—Named for the messenger of the gods who was incredibly fast, this planet revolves around the sun faster than all other planets.

VENUS—This planet was named after the goddess of love. Venus is one of the brightest objects in the night sky.

MARS—This planet was named for the god of war because of its angry red color.

JUPITER—The largest of the planets is named after the Roman ruler of the gods.

SATURN—The god Saturn was the god of time.

URANUS—This planet was named after the father of the Greek Titans.

NEPTUNE—The god Neptune was ruler of the sea.

PLUTO—In Greek mythology, Pluto was ruler of the underworld. Although it is a dwarf planet due partly to its small size, Pluto has several moons with mythic names: Charon, the ferryman of the River Styx; Nix, goddess of the night; and Hydra, the nine-headed serpent that Heracles battles.

LOOK AT THE SKY

Other constellations are named for heroes and mythical characters. Try looking at the sky during a cloudless night and name your own constellation. Here are some well-known constellations:

ORION—A mighty hunter in myth, this constellation is easiest to see during the winter months and is most recognizable by the three bright stars that make up Orion's belt.

AQUILA—Zeus's eagle Aquila ate Prometheus's liver. This constellation is visible during the summer.

HERCULES—Some of the bravest heroes from myth, such as Hercules, were placed in the heavens by the gods as a way to honor them.

EXPLORER'S CORNER

Looking to the heavens, ancient people found reassurance in seeing the same patterns of stars over the years—probably because so many cosmic events, such as comets and eclipses, were frightening and unpredictable. These patterns of stars encouraged storytellers to see mythic creatures, such as Pegasus and Scorpio, and mythic heroes, such as Orion and Hercules, in constellations. Ancient peoples may have found it comforting to have their heroes up in the stars looking down upon them.

PHOTO FINISH

BEHIND THE ART WITH DR. ADRIENNE MAYOR

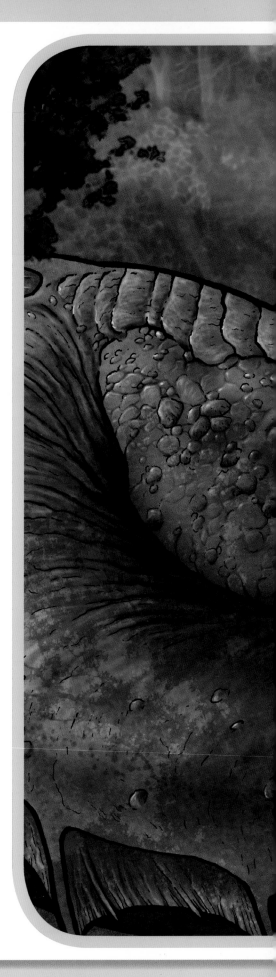

THIS COULD MORE CORRECTLY

BE CALLED AN "ART FINISH" AS THERE WASN'T photography back in ancient times. Instead, artists sculpted or painted images of mythological creatures. Some monsters were easy to portray because they were simply a combination of creatures, such as a woman-headed lion (Sphinx) or a bull-headed man (Minotaur). Others were more difficult to visualize as each artist had his own idea about what something such as a sea monster might look like. Did they have big eyes and toothy jaws? Did they have coils like a snake or a body more like a whale? Did they have legs or flippers? Were their tails like those of a fish or maybe a horse? The artists answered these questions in their work, and that led to there being many different variations of certain monsters, as well as different versions of some myths.

One of the most fascinating (and helpful) art forms is vase painting. Ancient Greek artists depicted scenes from myths, such as heroes battling monsters, on vases. People then were able to recognize the characters and creatures from the stories they enjoyed listening to. Those vases have also helped our modern-day understanding of ancient myths by providing details about stories and descriptions of monsters that were difficult to visualize from writings alone.

Today, if you visit just about any art museum, you can see sculptures and paintings that show mythological scenes, monsters, and heroes. They date back to ancient times and up to the modern day. Artists find myths just as inspiring as writers do.

Daniel Loxton's painting shows a scene from the Greek myth of Jason and the Argonauts and the quest for the Golden Fleece. Medea, a very powerful sorceress, helps Jason by using a sleeping potion to put Drakon, the monster guarding the fleece, to sleep. Loxton shows Drakon as a dragon, whereas ancient Greek vase paintings depict the monster as being a long, coiling serpent with a crocodile-like snout.

AFTERWORD

MYTHS HAVE BEEN AROUND
FOR THOUSANDS OF YEARS. BUT THEY NEVER

seem to get old. Today, we may rely on science to explain the world around us instead of telling myths about why it rains or how the world was created. And while we no longer worship mythic gods or fear the dreadful monsters from myths, mythology has forever affected the world around us, from influencing the books we read to providing exciting plots for the movies we watch.

Just look at the world around you, and you will see the many things in your everyday life that reference ancient myths. Ancient mythology surrounds us and influences our daily lives, from the sayings we use, almost without thinking, to the names of the cities and towns we live in today. We can't escape our pasts and the stories that were told to make sense of the world.

Cyclops—one of the X-Men, is a superhero who shoots a powerful red laser from his eyes. Like the Cyclops of ancient Greece, this superhero is considered a monster because of his powers.

TAKEN FROM MYTH

MEDUSA (Monster with snakes as hair in Greek mythology) The adult stage of a jellyfish

ATLAS (Titan who holds up the world) A book of maps

NIKE (Greek goddess of victory) A popular shoe and athletic clothing brand

CUPID (Roman god of love who carries a bow and arrow) A Valentine's Day symbol

MERCURY (Roman messenger of the gods) A liquid metal used in old thermometers that is sometimes called "quicksilver"

The sirens or mermaids of myth live on in movies, statues, and coffee shop logos. This one is a statue on a beach in southern Thailand.

The Trevi Fountain in Rome is a massive fountain that depicts the Roman god of the sea, Neptune, taming the waters with the help of Greek god Triton (son of Poseidon). Triton is taming the half-horse sea creature, the hippocampus.

POSITIS SIGNIS ET AN

POSITIS SIGNIS ET AN

AN INTERACTIVE GLOSSARY

WORDS OF THE GODS

The ancient Hindu god Hanuman is depicted as monkey-faced. He is swift, clever, and brave.

WANT TO LEARN MORE ABOUT THE

HEROES AND GODS BEHIND YOUR FAVORITE MYTHS? FIRST

muscle through this list of words you'll need to know and then see if you have mythic smarts. Afterward, check out the words in action on the pages listed.

1. Afterlife

Life after death; in myths, the afterlife is how a person's spirit continues on after it passes from its body. In most mythologies, a person's spirit travels to the underworld.
[PAGES 13, 27, 40–41]

Which is NOT a god of the afterlife?
a. Pluto
b. Freya
c. Anubis
d. Kashima-no-kami

2. Avatar

The manifestation of a god or spirit; avatars were one way for divine beings to interact with creatures on Earth. They would often appear as animals or people because to view their true form would be deadly to mortals. Also, by using avatars, gods would stay safe from harm even if their avatars were hurt.
[PAGE 14]

Which god is an avatar?
a. Thor
b. Hera
c. Ganesha
d. Neptune

3. Creator

The god or being that brought the world into existence
[PAGES 10, 16, 35, 36]

Which is NOT a creator god in myths?
a. Gaia
b. Heart of Sky
c. Horus
d. Great Ruler

4. Geomythology

The investigation of early, pre-science myths that show an understanding about natural phenomena, such as earthquakes, floods, tsunamis, and volcanoes
[PAGES 7, 38]

Which would be a geomyth?
a. The 12 Labors of Heracles
b. The story of the Minotaur
c. The story of Arachne
d. The tale of the giant catfish Namazu

5. Immortal

A god or being that is not subject to death and will live forever
[PAGES 15, 22]

Which of the following are immortals?
a. Thor
b. Cronus
c. Heracles
d. Prometheus

6. Mortal

Subject to death; people (and some gods) are mortals because they can die.
[PAGES 19, 23, 29, 36, 41, 50–51]

Which of the following are mortals?
a. Thor
b. Cronus
c. Heracles
d. Prometheus

7. Pantheon

All the gods in one mythology or religion
[PAGES 22, 50]

Of the most common modern religions, which one has a pantheon?
a. Christianity
b. Hinduism
c. Islam
d. Judaism

8. Quest

A long journey, often to a strange and faraway land, that a hero undertakes; heroes usually go on their quests to battle fearsome beasts or to help people, or both.
[PAGES 11, 28, 31, 47]

Who would most likely go on a quest?
a. Odin
b. Athena
c. Bellerophon
d. Garuda

9. Spirit

The manifestation of a godlike creature on Earth; spirits often take the form of an animal in order to communicate with people. In most mythologies, they are not as powerful as true gods.
[PAGES 10, 12–13, 16–17, 34]

Which of the following creatures was considered a "spirit"?
a. Perseus
b. Beaver
c. Shiva
d. Thor

10. Temple

A building devoted to the worship of a god or gods
[PAGES 4–5, 12–13, 26]

Ancient peoples had many sacred places in which they worshipped their gods. Which of these was a temple?
a. Cholula Pyramid
b. Uluru
c. Valley of the Kings
d. Mount Olympus

11. Trickster

A god or spirit who is often deceitful or likes to play tricks; some tricksters were said to help people while others liked to fool them.
[PAGES 15, 17, 34–35]

Of the various trickster gods and spirits, which one was most likely to harm people?
a. Coyote
b. Prometheus
c. Loki
d. Anansi

12. Underworld

The realm in myths where the dead go; often the underworld is seen as a physical world that exists below the Earth.
[PAGES 19, 29, 30, 40–41, 47, 53]

Like the world aboveground, the underworld is made up of several places. Which is a place NOT found in the underworld?
a. Elysian Fields
b. Angkor Wat
c. The River Acheron
d. Tartarus

ANSWERS:
1. d; 2. c; 3. c; 4. d; 5. b and c; 6. a and c; 7. b; 8. c; 9. b; 10. a; 11. c; 12. b

FIND OUT MORE

Extend your stay in the world of ancient myths with these books, movies, and more.

FESTIVALS

Chinese New Year is usually celebrated in mid-January to honor ancestors and gods.

Day of the Dead, a Mexican holiday held November 1, has its roots in an Aztec festival honoring the goddess of the underworld.

Diwali, the Hindu festival of lights, is a four-day festival that honors several gods.

MOVIES*

Harry Potter and the Sorcerer's Stone
Warner Brothers Pictures, 2001

Iron Man
Paramount Pictures, 2008

Man of Steel
Warner Brothers Pictures, 2013

Percy Jackson and the Olympians: The Lightning Thief
Twentieth Century Fox, 2010

Percy Jackson: Sea of Monsters
Twentieth Century Fox, 2013

Thor
Paramount Pictures, 2011

X-Men
Twentieth Century Fox, 2000

* Ask a parent for permission to watch these movies.

MYTHICALLY GOOD BOOKS

Oh My Gods!: A Look-It-Up Guide to the Gods of Mythology
Megan E. Bryant
Franklin Watts, 2009

Treasury of Greek Mythology: Classic Stories of Gods, Goddesses, Heroes & Monsters
Donna Jo Napoli
National Geographic Society, 2011

MYTHIC PLACES TO VISIT

Angkor Wat Angkor Wat, Cambodia

The Pantheon Rome, Italy

The Parthenon on the Acropolis Athens, Greece

Valley of the Kings Luxor, Egypt

Published by the National Geographic Society

John M. Fahey, *Chairman of the Board and Chief Executive Officer*

Declan Moore, *Executive Vice President; President, Publishing and Travel*

Melina Gerosa Bellows, *Executive Vice President; Chief Creative Officer, Books, Kids, and Family*

Prepared by the Book Division

Hector Sierra, *Senior Vice President and General Manager*

Nancy Laties Feresten, *Senior Vice President, Kids Publishing and Media*

Jennifer Emmett, *Vice President, Editorial Director, Children's Books*

Eva Absher-Schantz, *Design Director, Kids Publishing and Media*

Jay Sumner, *Director of Photography, Children's Publishing*

R. Gary Colbert, *Production Director*

Jennifer A. Thornton, *Director of Managing Editorial*

NG Staff for This Book

Robin Terry, *Project Editor*

James Hiscott, Jr., *Art Director*

Lori Epstein, *Senior Photo Editor*

Ariane Szu-Tu, *Editorial Assistant*

Callie Broaddus, *Design Production Assistant*

Margaret Leist, *Photo Assistant*

Carl Mehler, *Director of Maps*

Grace Hill, *Associate Managing Editor*

Joan Gossett, *Production Editor*

Lewis R. Bassford, *Production Manager*

Susan Borke, *Legal and Business Affairs*

Production Services

Phillip L. Schlosser, *Senior Vice President*

Chris Brown, *Vice President, NG Book Manufacturing*

George Bounelis, *Senior Production Manager*

Nicole Elliott, *Director of Production*

Rachel Faulise, *Manager*

Robert L. Barr, *Manager*

Editorial, Design, and Production by Plan B Book Packagers

Captions

Cover: Poseidon, Greek god of the sea

Back cover: (left) A Balinese god mask (right) Neptune was the Roman god of water and the sea.

Page 1: Thor, the Viking god of thunder, wields his mighty magic hammer against a giant.

Page 2: One of the best known stories of myth is of the Greek hero Perseus and the Gorgon Medusa. Perseus was sent to slay Medusa, a snake-headed monster who turned all who looked at her to stone.

The National Geographic Society is one of the world's largest nonprofit scientific and educational organizations. Founded in 1888 to "increase and diffuse geographic knowledge," the Society works to inspire people to care about the planet. National Geographic reflects the world through its magazines, television programs, films, music and radio, books, DVDs, maps, exhibitions, live events, school publishing programs, interactive media and merchandise. *National Geographic* magazine, the Society's official journal, published in English and 38 local-language editions, is read by more than 60 million people each month. The National Geographic Channel reaches 320 million households in 38 languages in 171 countries. National Geographic Digital Media receives more than 25 million visitors a month. National Geographic has funded more than 10,000 scientific research, conservation and exploration projects and supports an education program promoting geographic literacy.

For more information, please visit www.nationalgeographic.com, call 1-800-NGS LINE (647-5463), or write to the following address:
National Geographic Society
1145 17th Street N.W.
Washington, D.C. 20036-4688 U.S.A.

Visit us online at www.nationalgeographic.com/books

For librarians and teachers: www.ngchildrensbooks.org

More for kids from National Geographic:
kids.nationalgeographic.com

For information about special discounts for bulk purchases, please contact National Geographic Books Special Sales: ngspecsales@ngs.org

For rights or permissions inquiries, please contact National Geographic Books Subsidiary Rights: ngbookrights@ngs.org

Paperback ISBN: 978-1-4263-1498-8
Reinfored library binding ISBN: 978-1-4263-1499-5

Printed in Hong Kong
14/THK/1